CROSSROADS, INTERSECTIONS, & JUNCTIONS

Dr. Juan M. Brown, Sr.

To Delano Blackwell,

My true friend and brother

in the faith who is at a crossroad

in his life, lying in a hospital bed and in

need of a miracle from God.

CONTENTS

Introduction

CROSSROADS, INTERSECTIONS, & JUNCTIONS

Let's look at some terminology from a spiritual perspective:

The definition of a crossroad.

The definition of an intersection.

The definition of a junction.

What is a Crossroad?

A crossroad is a point in time whereby the Holy Spirit of God brings you to a place in life where change is imminent and critical decisions must be made. It means God is getting ready to move in an unprecedented way in your life. It means God is so ready to shift you from where you are to where He wants you to be. Simply put, it means God is getting ready to take you in a new direction. How exciting is that? Who does that? Only the God we serve can do such great things as to change the time, season, and direction at certain points in your life. You should be praising Him right about now! Resist being angry, worried or stressed. God is about to do something greater with you as He always done so in the lives of His people. It is at this time when God fills you with an expectation that is from Him, so then you should be filled with anticipation that something good is going to happen next.

What is an Intersection?

An intersection is a crossing or a time of crossing. Intersections force you to make decisions and turns at the right time. You have been traveling for so long with God in a particular season and direction that you have gotten comfortable and have accomplished all that He has set out to do in your life. He brings you to an intersection or to another aspect of His will for your life. You are influenced by the Holy Spirit to make this transition, or to make the move necessary to accommodate His plan for your life.

Any other moment in time you may not have even thought about God's next move for one reason or the other, but intersections in life also causes us to pause, pray, and seek God's will. It suggests that there is more for you on the journey and that God is not done with you yet. Greater is always next on God's agenda. He never makes lateral moves, same level moves, or backward moves in our lives. If you follow the Holy Spirit's signals at this point, He will lead you across the intersection safe and sound to experience the best in life that God has to offer.

What is a Junction?

A junction is where roads or paths meet. Junctions connect you to the next road that will ultimately lead you to your place of purpose where God wants you to be. I promise you will encounter intersections, crossroads, junctions, and other varied roads and traffic systems on your way to the center of God's will. The types of road junctions you will run into will vary from time to time and season to season.

There are unmarked, marked, and controlled junctions, etc. Understanding how to deal with each type of junction is not only essential for safe driving, but also important for arriving spirit-filled and intact to your destiny. You don't always have to wreck in life to get on the road that leads to the fulfillment of God's purpose. You can merge smoothly from grace to grace and from place to place. Crosswords, intersections, and junctions are one of several indicators that let you and I know that God is up to something good for us that will bring Him glory.

Understanding what God is up too when we come to a crossroad.

While driving, we all have come to a crossroad; a turning point in the road that directs us to turn, cross, or exit at some point in our driving experience. Whichever may be the case, when we came to that point in the road there are also signs, signals, flashing lights, barriers, road guards, or even policemen on that section of the highway to give us specific directions as to what to do next.

In all my years of experience in driving, I have come upon many crossroads, intersections, and junctions. I have seen people going through a gambit of poignant emotions due to being in a rush to get from point "A" to point "B." For many of these drivers, including myself at times, these were frustrating moments while trying to navigate the way to one's desired destination.

Turns in the road, early exits, stop lights, slow down signals, turn right, and turn left, waves, barricades, signalmen, policemen, are all there to assist privileged drivers to make the right decision at the critical time of crossing. Look at all the help we have at intersections on our highways in the United States.

You and I never know what is ahead or what is at a particular section of the road, such as an accident, construction, and oncoming traffic, a disabled vehicle and, in some cases, a casualty that merits our having to slow down and go in another direction.

A crossroad forces us to go in another direction on the highway even when we do not want to. Let's tell the truth and shame the devil; most of us just want to get to where we are trying to go as fast as we can and do not want anything impeding our travels along the way. What happens when you come to a crossroad on the roadway forcing you to decide?

It is decision-making time. What you do next will determine if you will reach your destination. Well, so it is with crossroads in life! We all get to that point where it is time for a change, time to go in another direction, and time to make important decisions that will change the course and direction of our lives.

What you do at each crossroad in life will determine a lot. It will determine your happiness. It will determine your new start. It will determine how smooth your path will be. It will determine your attitude and how far you will go, etc.

Many times, people get beside themselves at critical points in the road to their destiny. It makes one wonder if they are ready for what is next in their life. Listen! Whenever God brings you and I to a crossroad, intersection, or junction in life it means one thing: He is about to change the course of your life. How exciting is that? According to Daniel 2:21a, the Bible says, "He is the God that changes times and seasons."

Get ready for some changes in the road.

Get ready for some turns in the road.

Get ready to exit one road to enter on to another road.

That is a good thing and not a bad thing. So, the Holy Spirit stops you in your tracks, causes you to slow down, prompts you to rethink, regroup, reorganize, reprioritize, and even repent, because major change is about to take place in your life. To run red lights, disregard yield signs, disobey signalmen, bust through barriers, exceed the speed limit at an intersection or junction, you do these at your own risk in the natural sense as well as the spiritual sense.

It would benefit you and I a great deal if we would possess a certain grace when we find ourselves at a crossroad in this journey called life, especially where we are at this stage in our walk with God after so many years, right? Honestly, you and I will have a few crossroads in which to face. And when we do, we need to be positioned properly, thinking straight with the mind of Christ, willing and ready to cooperate with the commands of the Holy Spirit. We must be sober-minded giving God our undivided attention with little to no distractions on the way to our destiny in Christ.

Even our heroes of faith faced challenges on the road to their appointment with destiny, but God seemed to always use the various drawbacks and trials to catapult them to their next destination.

God used a mountain and told Abraham it was time to move in another direction. God used the Red Sea to indicate to Moses and the Children of Israel it was time turn. In the Life of Joshua and the new generation of the Israelites, God used the Jordan River to specify that it was time to cross over. Joseph was thrown in a pit, but this wasn't any old pit. God used the pit as a crossroad to the palace. God uses various trials, situations and circumstances in our lives to get us moving, just as He did in biblical times with our favorite Bible characters.

Let us get ready for the next exciting journey on the road with the Lord. There are three things you need to remember when you encounter a crossroad, intersection, or junction from a spiritual standpoint:

1. **God is not trying to harm you.**

2. **God is not trying to abandon you.**

3. **God will never leave you to navigate life's crossroads alone.**

Chapter 1

The Israelites

Going Back to Egypt is Not an Option

There is a sign on the road to your destiny that says, "Don't panic." Often- times when we run into what appears to be blocks in the road preventing us from going somewhere or entering a certain place, we panic and want to turn around and go back. Suddenly, where we have come from seems more attractive than where we were headed to because of the perceived jams on the road slowing us down or outright shutting us off from our objective.

What happens next? Trepidation sets in and we react to the conditions around us. In most cases, human nature just kicks in and says, "Turn around and go back home!" I say to you today going back is not an option.

I recall as a child growing up in Los Angeles seeing my mother's determination to provide a better life for my siblings and me. She worked in the Beverly Hills area, which is a suburb of Los Angeles, where she cleaned houses from sun up to sundown. My mother would come home, cook, clean, feed the family, get us ready for the next day of school, and tuck us into bed. Then Mother Brown would take a break from the entire day, which seemed to be for just a few minutes, all to get back up and repeat the routine the next day.

There were times I'd see my mother in pain and crying from the arduous workload that day, but she kept on pressing forward because she was dead set on giving us a better life. She would work as a housemaid for a few years until another opportunity arose. It was as if God placed an opening before her, but that new start came with a new set of challenges, as does every new opportunity in life. I remember my dear mother expressing to us as a family how scared she was and how she felt that she wasn't qualified for the new position. I forgot to mention the window of opportunity came from a person whose house she was cleaning at the time, who happened to be the president of the Aerospace Corporation. He liked my mother's work so much that he wanted to hire her as the maintenance engineer of the corporation. The opportunity did not come without critics, jealousy, envy from others, and even prejudice. However, my mother went forward despite the bumps in the road ahead.

In addition, to make life more challenging, my mother was a single parent, rearing three children in one of the roughest places in Los Angeles, but here is what I heard my mother saying, "Going back was not an option." She saw the challenges in front of her, assessed the challenges behind her, weighed all the opposing factors and continued moving forward because she decided going back to cleaning other people's houses was not an option. She felt that God had something greater in store for her family. I saw this attitude in my mother at an incredibly young age and it was the very first place I learned the importance of not giving up. My mother felt like whatever she had to face moving forward was worth more than where she had come from. God was about to elevate her and going back was not an option.

Quite possibly what you are facing in the road is not absolute or definite, but it is a crossroad. It is designed by God to slow you down for the next turn your life is about to take. Those that come to mind are the Children of Israel as they faced the Red Sea. After God delivered them from four hundred years of slavery in Egypt, they come to a Red Sea situation. The Red Sea was an elongated body of water located in the Middle East. It was an Inland Sea, which meant it was largely enclosed by the mainland. The land on both sides was mostly desert. I am sure at this point in the journey the Children of Israel were perplexed, baffled, and puzzled as they looked toward the Red Sea and saw Pharaoh and his army chasing them.

"When Pharaoh drew near, the people of Israel lifted their eyes, and behold, the Egyptians were marching after them, and they feared greatly. And the people of Israel cried out to the LORD. They said to Moses, is it because there are no graves in Egypt that you have taken us away to die in the wilderness? What have you done to us in bringing us out of Egypt? Is not this what we said to you in Egypt: Leave us alone that we may serve the Egyptians. For it would have been better for us to serve the Egyptians than to die in the wilderness." (Exodus 14:9-12)

As the Lord met the Israelites at the Red Sea, they began to panic. Why? They concluded that the Red Sea was a drawback and deterrent to the land of promise. But, in all actuality, it was just an intersection that God was going to use to turn them towards a greater place: The

Promised Land. The Children of Israel wanted to go back to Egypt but, according to God's will, that was not an option. Neither is it an option for us today as we face our own crossroads, intersections, and junctions in life. Do you hear me?

Three things I learned from my mother's testimony and the text before us.

Face What Faces You

The Lord instructed Moses, "tell the people to turn towards Pihahiroth between Migdol and the sea, opposite Baal Zephan, and to camp there along the shore." (Exodus 14:1-2)

Remember, going back to Egypt is not an option! God gives a mandate to the people to face the Red Sea and to camp there for a while. The Israelites had to face what was facing them. This huge body of water, which was approximately 1,398 miles in length, 220 miles in width, with a depth of 1,608 feet. Notice, God never told them to face Pharaoh and his army of six hundred chariots and the other chariots driven by the Egyptian officers. As they sojourned, there were new hills and hurdles in which to conquer. They had to face what was facing them, the Red Sea. They did not want to face it!

At any given crossroad, intersection, or junction in one's daily life experiences there will be things and people you must face to possess that which God has promised you. Usually, what God has ahead of us is much bigger and more substantial (the Red Sea) than what is behind us (Pharaoh and his army). Therefore, what God has in store for the future (His purpose, prosperity, peace, promises, etc.) is far greater than what is behind us.

What is keeping you from facing what faces you? Fear of the unknown, lack of confidence, lack of knowledge, lack of experience, low self-esteem, a comfort zone you are in, intimidation, a deficiency in a certain area of your life, or a lack of acceptance? Whatever it is, face it today in Jesus' name, knowing that "greater is He that is in you than He that is in the world." (1 John 4:4). God in his infinite wisdom instructed Moses to tell the people to turn towards the sea and encamp there, suggesting the idea that if God brought you to it, He will bring you through it!

Just as David had to face Goliath, Gideon had to face thousands of enemy troops, Daniel had to face the lions in the lion's den, and the Children of Israel would ultimately have to face the Red Sea, you and I must face what faces us at the critical point of change and challenges in our lives.

Stop Fussing

They said to Moses, "Is it because there are no graves in Egypt that you have taken us away to die in the wilderness? What have you done to us in bringing us out of Egypt? Is not this what we said to you in Egypt: 'Leave us alone that we may serve the Egyptians'? For it would have been better for us to serve the Egyptians than to die in the wilderness." (Exodus 14:11-12)

Blah! Blah! Blah! Pessimism set in at one of the greatest moments in the lives of the Israelites. They were at a crossroad, which meant God was about to do something big and here they are fussing at God and Moses. Look what they said, "You brought us this far out to die? Why did you have to bring us out of Egypt in the first place? We had it better in Egypt than where you have brought us." Isn't it amazing how the people whom God delivered would rather go back to bondage (what they were familiar with) because of perceived challenges rather than move forward into God's promises?

So, they fussed and complained the entire journey. They wanted to go back to Egypt regardless. Watch this! The work that the Egyptians forced on the Israelites was evil in motive and cruel in nature. The text says that the Egyptian masters worked the Israelites "ruthlessly" (Exodus 1:13-14) and made their lives "bitter" (Exodus 1:14) with "hard service" (Exodus 1:14; 6:9). As a result, Israel languished in "misery" and "suffering" (Exodus 3:7) and a "broken spirit" (Exodus 6:9). They wanted to return to the place that brought them so much pain rather than to enter the promises of God to bless and prosper them.

Sounds like something we would do as well; fuss with God while at a major intersection in life because there are some obstacles in the road. So, we contend with God to take us back to what was well known rather than to face the unknown (future). Here is what fussing on the journey does: it corrupts your spirit, it sets the mood of your atmosphere, it dictates your frame of mind, and it puts you in a bad position while you are waiting on God's next move. When you find yourself at a crossroad, intersection, or junction in life waiting on the Lord's next move, you will need to stay ready and in position full of faith and great expectation. Fussing and cussing removes you from the position where God needs you to be. David told us how we need to position ourselves:

Wait on the Lord be of good courage, and He shall strengthen your heart: wait, I say on the Lord. (Psalm 27:14)

Find your place of peace as God gets ready to make some major turns!

Go Forward

And Moses said to the people, "Fear not, stand firm, and see the salvation of the LORD, which he will work for you today. For the Egyptians whom you see today, you shall never see again. The LORD will fight for you, and you have only to be silent." The LORD said to Moses, "Why do you cry to me? Tell the people of Israel to go forward. (Exodus 14:13-15)

When the time comes to make the next turn, don't let fear grip your heart, stand and face what is facing you, and watch God work. Where do we go from this point? Forward! Knowing at least three things:

1. God has already worked it out (v.13b).

2. The Lord will fight for you (v.14).

3. He will talk you through it (v.15).

The natural thing to do is to turn around and go back; however, the supernatural thing to do is to advance even when you do not know what is ahead. You are now in the exact place God needs you to be to see Him work. God wanted them to see his salvation or His plan to make a way. Notice what Moses said to them at this point:

"Fear not, stand firm, and see the salvation of the LORD, which he will work for you today. For the Egyptians whom you see today, you shall never see again. The LORD will fight for you, so hold your peace." (Exodus 14:13-14)

What God has for you is ahead of you and no longer behind you. This was the perfect situation for the Children of Israel to see the hand of God probably for the first time. So, here they are at the Red Sea, a major turning point and they don't have a clue what God is about to do. Moses didn't even know what was next. The Lord was about to do it big in their lives and He wanted their attention fixed ahead of them. Look what happens next, God told Moses:

"Why do you cry to me? Tell the people of Israel to go forward. Lift your staff and stretch out your hand over the sea and divide it, that the people of Israel may go through the sea on dry ground." (Exodus 14:15-16)

God is not done, watch the text:

"And I will harden the hearts of the Egyptians so that they shall go in after them, and I will get glory over Pharaoh and all his host, his chariots, and his horsemen. And the Egyptians shall know that I am the LORD, when I have gotten glory over Pharaoh, his chariots, and his horsemen. Then the angel of God who was going before the host of Israel moved and went behind them, and the pillar of cloud moved from before them and stood behind them, coming between the host of Egypt and the host of Israel. And there was the cloud and the darkness.

And it lit up the night without one coming near the other all night." (Exodus 14:17-20)

Moses, still not sure what God is up to, but he is obedient to God at this crossroad in life and look what happens:

Then Moses stretched out his hand over the sea, and the LORD drove the sea back by a strong east wind all night and made the sea dry land, and the waters were divided. And the people of Israel went into the midst of the sea on dry ground, the waters being a wall to them on their right hand and on their left. (Exodus 14:21-22)

What God starts He always finishes. He shuts the door on the past:

The Egyptians pursued and went in after them into the midst of the sea, all Pharaoh's horses, his chariots, and his horsemen. And in the morning watch the LORD in the pillar of fire and of cloud looked down on the Egyptian forces and threw the Egyptian forces into a panic, clogging their chariot wheels so that they drove heavily. And the Egyptians said, "Let us flee from before Israel, for the LORD fights for them against the Egyptians." Then the LORD said to Moses, "Stretch out your hand over the sea, that the water may come back upon the Egyptians, upon their chariots, and upon their horsemen. So, Moses stretched out his hand over the sea, and the sea returned to its normal course when the morning appeared. And as the Egyptians fled into it, the LORD threw the Egyptians into the midst of the sea. The waters returned and covered the chariots and the horsemen; of all the host of Pharaoh that had followed them into the sea, not one of them remained. (Exodus 14:23-28)

God has the outcome in His hand and His outcome is always good. Watch and see. He opens the door to the future:

But the people of Israel walked on dry ground through the sea, the waters being a wall to them on their right hand and on their left. Thus, the LORD saved Israel that day from the hand of the Egyptians, and Israel saw the Egyptians dead on the seashore. Israel saw the great power that the LORD used against the Egyptians, so the people feared the LORD, and they believed in the LORD and in his servant Moses. (Exodus 14:29-31)

Just think had the Israelites turned back to Egypt they would have missed out on one of the greatest experiences in their lives. In addition, they would have continued to be stuck in a life of bondage. What God had for Israel required them to go forward. So, it is with you and I. Onward we must go if we are going to see the wonderful things God has planned and purposed for our lives. Do it scared and never turn back. There's nothing wrong with being afraid, but never allow your fears to keep you from where God is leading you.

Chapter 2

Abraham

It is Time to Move

Now that you have made up your mind that going back regardless of the crossroad in front is not an option, let us prepare our hearts and minds to listen actively to the Holy Spirit's direction to take us further up the road to destiny. Whenever God brings you and I to a crossroad, intersection, or junction in life, He is telling us it is time to move. God begins to make gestures to express that it is time to proceed or advance by bringing you to a point in the road where you will need His power, wisdom and guidance. Usually it is the bends, the curves and the loops in the road that begin to slow you down first, then you find yourself at a dead end from which no exit is possible. You, my friend, are at a crossroad in life and the Lord could possibly be telling you that it is time to move. You have been in the same place in your life long enough that you have completed what you were supposed to do or perhaps you have outgrown where you are. God has fulfilled all that He had planned and purposed you to do. There comes a time when He simply says, "Move!" Crossroads, intersections, and junctions advise you that God is about to make a major revision in your life once again. This could be exciting or not depending upon how you view change!

I recall an experience the Holy Spirit afforded me years ago while I was in my twenties. It was both a frightening and exciting gesture from the Lord as He motioned to me it was time to move from California to Arizona. Other than traveling around the world while serving in the military, I had never resided outside of California and had no plans to live anywhere else because all my family lived there. All my friends settled in various cities within the state. I received my education from the public school system in Los Angeles County in the state of California. Pridefully speaking, it is the golden state. At one point or another I had either lived in or visited all twelve regions of California. I knew all the tourist attractions, freeways, streets, desert areas, hills, and mountains.

Most of my church family were people that I grew up with and made California their home. I was a California native and had no intentions of ever changing my area code, right? However, the Lord had a different plan. It reminds me of when God told the prophet Isaiah:

"For my thoughts are not your thoughts, neither are your ways my ways, saith the Lord. For as the heavens are higher than the earth, so are my ways higher than your ways, and my thoughts than your thoughts." (Isaiah 55:8-9)

God had intentions on moving me from the place where I was born, reared and raised to a place I had never been. Little did I know at the time that it would be a huge move, a major move and one of the best moves ever in my life. Prior to the transfer from California to Arizona, I had encountered a few bends, curves and loops in the road that slowed me down from the fast-paced lifestyle I was living. Ultimately, I found myself at a crossroad again, in need of God's power, wisdom and guidance.

Things just started to happen to cause me to want to leave California. For example, my pastor died unexpectedly. I lost my way in the ministry. Other ministry doors and opportunities closed in my face. I lost my job and had to move my family and I back to my mother's home. Those were the bends in the road I was speaking of earlier and eventually I hit that dead end with no way to turn or move. I was at that crossroad, intersection, and junction in my life where I needed to hear from the Lord. I was exactly where God needed me to be in order to pay attention and listen to Him.

At that point, I was filled with mixed emotions. I was scared, agitated, nervous, intimidated, and I panicked because I didn't know what I was going to do. Then one day I received an invitation to preach as a candidate for the role of senior pastor at a church in Arizona. I went to preach and became a finalist in the process for candidacy for the role of senior pastor. I preached a second time and the rest is history. The church voted for me to be their new senior pastor. That meant my family and I were moving to Arizona. God has a way of moving us from one point to another. When you come across such turning points, you are at a critical point in life, which usually means from heaven's standpoint that it is time to move. It is time to advance because you have been in that place long enough. Abram (better known by his latter name Abraham), like you and I, had reached a crossroad in his life that meant God was about to do something huge. Abraham runs into some bends and twists in the road just before God calls him to be the father of many nations upon the earth.

Abraham's brother, Haran, dies at an early age in the land where he was born (in Ur of the Chaldeans). Lot, his nephew, who was a troubled child, came to live with Abraham and the family when his father, Haran, died.

Also, Abraham's brother, Nahor, ended up marrying his brother Haran's daughter, Milcah. Even Abraham married his half-sister, Sarai, who was barren and could not have children.

But God! He always uses the loops and curves to budge his people and that is what He is setting up to do in the life of Abraham.

Watch this!

Terah, the father of Abraham, decides to leave Ur of the Chaldeans to go to the land of Canaan. However, he stopped in the city of Haran and settled there instead. Terah settles for Haran over the land of Canaan which God would promise to His people. Terah dies there in Haran at the age of 205 years old. That was a lot for Abraham to deal with according to Genesis 11:26-32. You can always tell that God is up to something great when one of several things occurs in your life. At any given crossroad, intersection, or junction in life there will always be:

Trials

Abraham's brother, Haran, died at an early age and then his father, Terah, died leaving them in Haran (ref. to Genesis 11:28). Trials will show up in various ways and in some cases at a great loss, such as in the case of Abraham.

Tests

Sarai, his wife, was infertile and unable to produce children. Both Abram and Sarai were young and this would prove later to be a major problem that would affect his household and the world for that matter (ref. to Genesis 11:30). As believers, we will always be put to the test at our lowest and highest points in life. At certain points in the road, you are also vulnerable and at risk of the same trials and tests.

Temptation

Abram and Sarai fell to temptation when they deviated from God's game plan and proceeded to help God along in the fulfillment of His plan of action for the future. Sarai gave her Egyptian handmaid to Abram as a wife to bear him a child. Ishmael became Abram's firstborn son through Hagar, which was not God's plan. Temptation will always peak its head up at crossroads, intersections, and junctions to cause you to deviate from the purpose of God so that you might pursue your own methods and strategies (ref. Genesis 16:1-16).

Trouble

Abram was in trouble when he allowed his nephew, Lot, on the journey. God told him to leave your country, your people and your father's household (Ur of the Chaldeans, Haran), but he took Lot along for the trip (ref. Genesis 12:1, 4, 5). Lot was trouble! He proved to be more than a handful for Abram to oversee (ref. Genesis 13:1-18). Abram carried on what his father started when he took Lot into the household the first time.

The enemy strikes harder, right at the point of your crossing and moving into greater things the Lord has in store for you. Satan wants to destroy you, distract you, and dissuade you, right at the intersection where critical decisions and moves will be made. Always remember what Peter said:

"Beloved, think it not strange concerning the fiery trial among you, which cometh upon you to prove you, as though a strange thing happened unto you: but insomuch as ye are partakers of Christ's sufferings, rejoice; that at the revelation of his glory also ye may rejoice with exceeding joy." (I Peter 4:12-13)

Thus, Abram had a lot on his plate to deal with and now he is at a crossroad. Having taken up residence in Haran, it was time to move according to the word of the Lord. Haran was not God's intended place for them. Haran was a junction, or a meeting point that God used to begin the process of relocating Abram and his immediate family. His father took him so far, but it was just a start and now God calls Abram with a divine purpose in mind. It is time to move further on the road to destiny.

Perhaps where you are is not the place of God's purpose, but it is part of the journey that you should not despise but neither should you settle. Never park at a crossroad, intersection, or junction. Always keep your navigation system on in the spirit. However, you can certainly praise God while you are there waiting for the Holy Spirit's signal to lead you in the right direction. I promise if you wait, He will signal you which way to go. After the death of Abram's father, Go told him:

"Leave your own country (Haran) behind you, and your kinfolks and go to the land I will guide you to. If you do, I will cause you to become the father of a great nation; I will bless you and make your name famous, and you will be a blessing to many others. I will bless those who bless you and curse those who curse you; and the entire world will be blessed because of you." (Genesis 12:1-2)

On the other side of every crossroad, intersection and junction, awaiting you are the blessings of God if you can endure, keep going, do not tear up, and do not settle where you are. When it comes time to move, then move! God told Abram to move. It is time to proceed, it is time to go, it is time to advance beyond the city of Haran and into a place of greater, the land of Canaan. Isn't that just like the God we serve? He told Abram in Genesis 12 the following:

And I will make of thee a great nation, and I will bless thee, and make thy name great; and thou shalt be a blessing: And I will bless them that bless thee and curse him that cursed thee: and in thee shall all families of the earth be blessed. (Genesis 12:2-3)

All I can say is look at God! He never moves you just to move you. He tells you to proceed for a specific reason and it is never to waste your time or His time. Abram is about to be blessed beyond his imagination and all he must do at this junction is hold the line. Remember that crossroads, intersections, and junctions mean that God is about to shift you from where you are to where He purposed you to be for a particular season. Whenever He moves his people, it is always into greater things.

Look at what the psalmist said:

"The LORD shall increase you more and more, you and your children. Ye are blessed of the LORD which made heaven and earth." (Psalm 115:14-15)

To the Israelites God said:

"Hear, O Israel: Thou art to pass over Jordan this day, to go in to possess nations greater and mightier than thyself, cities great and fenced up to heaven…" (Deuteronomy 9:1)

To David God said:

"So, David became greater and greater: for the Lord of Host was with him." (1 Chronicles 11:9)

To Haggai God said:

"The glory of this latter house shall be greater than of the former, saith the LORD of hosts: and in this place will I give peace, saith the LORD of hosts." (Haggai 2:9)

To the believer's God said:

"But as it is written, Eye hath not seen, nor ear heard, neither have entered into the heart of man, the things which God hath prepared for them that love him." (1 Corinthians 2:9)

God always leads the way into the extraordinary and exceptional when he decides to move you as the scripture declares and reveals. So, it was at this crossroad (Haran) that God told Abram it is time to go. Notice what Abram does, the scripture says:

So, Abram departed, as the LORD had spoken unto him; and Lot went with him: and Abram was seventy-five years old when he departed out of Haran. And Abram took Sarai, his wife, and Lot his brother's son, and all their substance that they had gathered, and the souls that they had gotten in Haran; and they went forth to go into the land of Canaan; and into the land of Canaan, they came. (Genesis 12:4-5)

Abram, at the age of 75 years old got up from where his father settled, got his wife Sarai, packed up all their belongings, valuables, cattle, and servants he had gotten in Haran.

Abram permitted Lot to go with them. They left their homeland and finally arrived in Canaan. Abram moved when God said, "move." If you find yourself at a crossroad, intersection, or junction in your life experiences let me give you four suggestions that have helped me:

Get up!

Get dressed!

Show up!

Watch God work!

Get up from where you are, get yourself situated, and show up with confidence and boldness like you know God sent you. Watch God work favorably in your life. Thank God for every crossroad, intersection, and junction you encounter. It means God is getting ready to enlarge your territory and take you to a greater place. You should be excited!

Chapter 3

Moses

It is Time to Turn

In chapter two God told Abram that it was time to move. As Moses and the Children of Israel made their way out of Egypt, He told them to turn. That is, turn back around. Huh? Perhaps you are in a season where God may tell you to make such a turn. You will need to prepare your heart and your mind as the Holy Spirit takes you further up the road that leads to your place of purpose and greater blessings. Whenever God brings you to a crossroad, intersection, or junction in your life, He is telling you it is time to make a few turns as well. It is never to just stop you in traffic and leave you there all alone to figure out the next move. Also, turning involves merging into the next season of your life as safe as possible without disrupting God's plan or violently colliding into other people's lanes. In which many individuals do at this point in their journey. I see it all the time among Christians who are in a rush to get to their God given future. They will go barreling through stop signs and avoiding signals telling them to slow down, while ignoring blind spots. Now they are involved in a crash at another crossroad in life. I hope we will learn that all is well and greater is ahead in our crossing and merging.

I am a frequent driver on the road, especially for carrying out my daily pastoral duties and traveling with loved ones for family fun and vacations. I remember on one occasion coming to an intersection in the road and there was a policeman directing me to turn. At that point, I did not understand why I had to make the turn that was not part of the travel plan. I got so frustrated, panic set in because I was going to be late to my destination. I did not understand the policeman telling me the reason I had to turn because I wanted my way and I had not anticipated any delays on the road. Can you imagine going through these emotions and unsettling thoughts with the Holy Spirit over a simple turn that He needs us to make in order to get us closer to the center of God's will for our lives? I made the turn as directed by the policeman, all to discover later the reason for the turn at that junction in the road; city workers were improving the street for better mobility for drivers and pedestrians. Really! All the fuss and anguish were for nothing and turning wasn't that bad after all. So, it is with God, in the realm of the spirit when He directs us to turn in life, it is always for our good. God is always in the process of improving the infrastructure of our lives, and making the right turns in our walk becomes an important factor.

We come to the story of Moses and the Children of Israel again. It was time for them to turn, watch the text:

The Lord instructed Moses, "tell the people to turn towards Pihahiroth between Migdol and the sea, opposite Baal Zephan, and to camp there along the shore." (Exodus 14:1-2)

Moses and the Children of Israel had reached an intersection and by now God had already delivered the people in Egypt from the hand of Pharaoh.

As they struggled not to go back to Egypt and to push forward, they'd have to make one of the most important moves in the journey. They'd have to turn! Turn where? Northward. In other words, they were instructed to turn back. Yes, turn back! I couldn't believe it when I read it. After a couple of pitstops in a southerly direction away from Egypt (ref. Exodus 13:18, 20), God instructs Moses to tell the people to turn back in the general direction from which they had come. The directive was crystal clear. They were to go back to Egypt, and God would lead His people around by the desert, then toward the Red Sea, which was the longer route to their intended destination.

God could have taken the Israelites a shorter way:

"When Pharaoh let the people go, God did not lead them by way of the land of the Philistines, although that was nearby. For God said, Lest the people change their minds when they see war and return to Egypt.

But God led the people around by the way of the wilderness toward the Red Sea…even though they had left Egypt armed." (Exodus 13:17-18)

Instead of leading the Children of Israel southward through Philistine territory, which was a direct route to Canaan (the Promised Land), but heavily guarded by an Egyptian military stronghold, God decides not to take them down that road. He told them to turn northward to a desert road that would lead them to the Red Sea instead. Then they were to stop and camp out for a while. With Pharaoh and his army in hot pursuit, the Lord would be a shield (ref. Exodus 13:20-22) for His people up to the actual crossing over the Red Sea. Subsequently, God would tell them to turn around and the Shield of the Lord would come down (ref. Exodus 14:4, 8-10) leaving Israel vulnerable to the enemy behind them and a large body of water in front of them. The chase is back in full motion, and it could have ended back in chapter thirteen had they taken the shorter pathway through Philistine territory.

When you come to a crossroad, intersection, or junction in life, making the precise turn becomes essential if you are going to get to the next season of your life. Having to turn to the right or to the left or even having to turn around to a degree at God's charge should not throw you off in your faith. Coming to a crossroad means God is trying to turn you in a precise direction for a specific reason. Inhale, exhale, calm down, and stay in faith because God is about to do something great in your life. He may tell you to do the same thing that He instructed Moses and the Israelites to do "turn."

So why would God tell Moses and the Children of Israel to turn back at this juncture? They had come so far, now they were being led to go back in the general direction from which they had come. Sometimes God will tell us to turn for several, very practical reasons.

To Protect Us

Wherever God leads, God protects! There will never be a time when we are outside of God's protection when we follow his directions. The Lord told Moses to tell the people to turn for their own protection. Little did Moses and the Children of Israel realize, the sea itself would be their protective shield in the end as it would come down upon the Egyptians, drowning them. (ref. Exodus 14:26-28). The water covered Pharaoh, his army, the chariots, and all their horses; not one of the

Egyptians remained alive. God will never tell us to make a move of any sort and leave us without His security. God promises His people:

"Be strong and courageous. Do not fear or be in dread of them, for it is the LORD your God who goes with you. He will not leave you or forsake you." (Deuteronomy 31:6)

Paul reminded the church at Thessalonica:

"But the Lord is faithful. He will establish you and guard you against the evil one." (2 Thessalonians 3:3)

David reminds us as the people of God:

"I lift up my eyes to the hills. From where does my help come? My help comes from the LORD, who made heaven and earth. He will not let your foot be moved; he who keeps you will not slumber. Behold, he who keeps Israel will neither slumber nor sleep. The LORD is your keeper; the LORD is your shade on your right hand. The sun shall not strike you by day, nor the moon by night. The LORD will keep you from all evil; he will keep your life. The LORD will keep you're going out and you're coming in from this time forth and forevermore." (Psalm 121:1-8)

You may feel in danger and unsafe at times, but you are never without God's assurance of care and safety.

To Preserve Us

Remember in Exodus 13:17-18 when Pharaoh initially released the Israelites from bondage in Egypt? God did not lead them through the land of the Philistines, although that was the most direct route. The

Lord felt they would become discouraged by having to fight their way through and that they would want to return to Egypt. The Children of Israel were exhausted. As frustrating as it was to have to fight the rest of the way may have proven to be of no effect. So, God took them by way of the wilderness having made a couple of turns before coming to the Red Sea. The necessary turns in the journey were for their preservation and conservation for the long trip ahead of them. The Lord never just sends us into the fire without His commitment to look after us. He knows what we can and cannot handle, so He puts us on certain roads in life that will best sustain us and not drain us before we get to our place of purpose. What good is it if we are worn out or bone-weary before we get to the next season? None! God keeps us, He knows exactly how to do it for us, and He needs no help from you or me.

David prayed for God to preserve him on many occasions:

"Deliver me, O LORD, from evil men; preserve me from violent men, who plan evil things in their heart and stir up wars continually. They make their tongue sharp as a serpent, and under their lips is the venom of asps. Selah Guard me, O LORD, from the hands of the wicked; preserve me from violent men, who have planned to trip up my feet." (Psalm 140:1-4)

Here is another promise regarding God preserving us:

"The LORD is your keeper; the LORD is your shade on your right hand. The sun shall not strike you by day, nor the moon by night. The LORD will keep you from all evil; he will keep your life. The LORD will keep your going out and you're coming in from this time forth and forevermore." (Psalm 121:4-8)

As children of God, we will never look like what we've been through because God preserves us through it all. Sometimes the Lord will instruct us to turn in order to preserve us and/or save us from both seen and unseen dangers.

To Prosper Us

God's moves in our lives are never lateral or same level moves. When He instructs us to turn it is always for the greater as it pertains to His will for our lives. All the moves and turns the Children of Israel would have to take was to ultimately lead them to a better place where they would prosper. The turn towards the Red Sea made no sense initially. Little did the Children of Israel know that God was going to actually use Pharaoh and his army to chase them in the direction where they would prosper. Yes! The enemy chased them closer to the land of promise and they didn't even know it.

Truth be told, sometimes God must use circumstances to get us up and moving because if He left it up to us, we would camp out along the wilderness seashore much too long and probably never get going. So, God changed Pharaoh's mind about releasing them and the chase was on. You may not understand in the first instance why this turn or why that turn, just know whenever God changes your route it is always for the greater good and never to harm you. Scripture teaches us some of the following:

"Beloved, I wish above all things that thou mayest prosper and be in health, even as thy soul prospers." (3 John 1:2)

"Let them shout for joy, and be glad, that favor my righteous cause: yea, let them say continually, Let the LORD be magnified, which hath pleasure in the prosperity of his servant." (Psalm 35:27)

"If ye be willing and obedient, ye shall eat the good of the land: But if ye refuse and rebel, ye shall be devoured by your enemies: for the mouth of the LORD hath spoken it." (Isaiah 1:19-20)

"For I know the plans I have for you, declares the Lord, plans to prosper you and not to harm you, plans to give you hope and a future." (Jeremiah 29:11)

God told Joshua:

"This book of the law shall not depart out of thy mouth; but thou shalt meditate therein day and night, that thou mayest observe to do according to all that is written therein: for then thou shalt make thy way prosperous, and then thou shalt have good success." (Joshua 1:8)

The Lord will tell you to turn in order to lead you into an extraordinary and exceptional life. The next time God tells you to turn back around or to simply turn in a certain direction, just do it! Think, He is expanding my life. He is enlarging my territory!

To Perplex the Enemy

God told Moses and the Children of Israel to turn back toward the Red Sea wilderness within enemy territory to baffle them into thinking that they had the upper hand:

"For Pharaoh will say of the children of Israel, they are entangled in the land, the wilderness hath shut them in. And I will harden Pharaoh's heart, that he shall follow after them; and I will be honored upon Pharaoh, and upon all his host; that the Egyptians may know that I am the LORD. And they did so." (Exodus 14:3-4)

Pharaoh said we got them now! He thought he had the upper hand, but in a very real sense, Pharaoh and his army were playing into God's hand. The enemy thought he had them cornered and trapped in the land and there was no escape. Pharaoh's plan was to retrieve them and bring them back to Egypt, including much of the wealth they took from Egypt (ref. Exodus 14:5-9). However, God confused the enemy to fulfill His plan and purpose for the Children of Israel. This can be one of the most fearful times in your life, when God tells you to make certain turns in a certain direction and you meet back up with the enemy. Panic sets in and fear begins to overtake you and you begin to cry out to the Lord. That is what the Children of Israel did:

"And when Pharaoh drew nigh, the children of Israel lifted up their eyes, and behold, the Egyptians marched after them; and they were sore afraid: and the children of Israel cried out unto the LORD." (Exodus 14:10)

Then they started to complain again:

"And they said unto Moses, because there were no graves in Egypt, hast thou taken us away to die in the wilderness? Wherefore hast thou dealt thus with us, to carry us forth out of Egypt? Is not this the word that we did tell thee in Egypt, saying, let us alone, that we may serve the Egyptians? For it had been better for us to serve the Egyptians, than that we should die in the wilderness." (Exodus 14:11-12)

Then Moses told them:

"Fear ye not, stand still, and see the salvation of the LORD, which he will shew to you today: for the Egyptians whom ye have seen today, ye shall see them again no more forever. The LORD shall fight for you, and ye shall hold your peace." (Exodus 14:13-14)

God used the enemy to fulfill His purpose. When you see the enemy getting close and it appears he has the upper hand:

Do not fret.

Do not freeze.

Do not lose focus.

God is still working on your behalf even when the enemy is nearby. God is using the devil, your critics, your haters, all of your onlookers, etc., as part of His plan to give you the push you need. They are not even aware of it, but you are because of what the Word of God says about your enemies.

No matter what the devil and your enemies think about you, read what David says about them:

"I will call upon the LORD, who is worthy to be praised: so, shall I be saved from mine enemies." (Psalm 18:3)

"Thou hast also given me the necks of my enemies; that I might destroy them that hate me." (Psalm 18:40)

"He delivered me from my enemies: yea, He lifts me up above those that rise up against me: thou hast delivered me from the violent man." (Psalm 18:48)

The enemy may think he's got you! That is precisely what God wants him to believe about you. In essence, it is a set up to defeat the adversary and a means to launch you forward into your divine destiny. I hope you are getting it at this point. Making turns, especially unexpected turns, are an essential part of the journey if one has an inclination for fulfilling God's purpose.

For God to Get the Praise

God wants all to know that He is the Lord, including the enemy who seeks to throw you off at each crossroad, intersection, and junction you encounter. Ultimately, the Lord planned and allowed Pharaoh to chase Moses and the Children of Israel between Migdol and the Red Sea to gain great honor and glory over Pharaoh and all his armies. He wanted them to know that He is the Lord, the one and only Lord over all and above all:

"And I will harden Pharaoh's heart, that he shall follow after them; and I will be honored upon Pharaoh, and upon all his host; that the Egyptians may know that I am the LORD. And they did so." (Exodus 14:4)

Just think if Moses and the Children of Israel took the turn by way of the Philistines, which was nearer to their place of purpose, they could have attributed their success perhaps to themselves. Also, turning towards the land of the Philistines meant having to battle their way through even though they left Egypt well-armed to fight, it didn't happen! (ref. Exodus 13:17-18)

God did not want Israel to get discouraged having to fight their way through Philistine territory.

God would get more glory and honor taking them on an alternate route by way of the wilderness and the Red Sea.

Many times, we confront such bends in the road so that God will get the praise when it is all said and done. The long, roundabout route is not just for our protection, preservation, or to perplex the enemy, but for God to get the praise as we see Him work in our daily life experiences. When He tells you to turn, turn around, or go around, and you run into even greater obstacles, it is for the purpose of God's glory as He leads us into greater victories. The good news is this: Our Lord will never tell us to take a turn to our detriment, but it will always be for getting us to our destiny in the most triumphant way. Forward we go, no matter what lies ahead there is no time to waste, you have an appointment with destiny, and you can't be late.

Finally, Moses told the people:

"And Moses said unto the people, Fear ye not, stand still, and see the salvation of the LORD, which he will shew to you today: for the Egyptians whom ye have seen today, ye shall see them again no more forever. The LORD shall fight for you, and ye shall hold your peace." (Exodus 14:13-14)

Make sure that when God does it for you, give Him all the praise. Point to the Lord for each victory because it is God that fights all your battles on the way to your place of purpose.

As this chapter comes to an end, here are a few ways you can tell if it is God nudging you to turn vs. your inward fears or the suggestions of others:

Listen to the Voice of God

God will communicate one of several ways to let you know that it is time to make a definite turn at a particular time. He always communicates primarily through His Word. Secondly, He communicates through the indwelling of the Holy Spirit. God will communicate through your daily circumstances that it is expedient for you to turn now in a new direction in your life. God also articulates using the persuasion or a word from other people that know you and have your best interest in mind. Sometimes He will give you the idea, desire, or a mere impulse that it is time for a change. This is the litmus test to hearing the voice of God. He will keep imparting information until you get it and do it. Whichever way the Lord chooses to speak into your life, you will know that it is Him because it will challenge your faith, it will go against the grain of your own thinking, it will be consistent with His written Word, it will require courage, and it will conflict with ungodly nature.

Recognize the Hand of God

God will begin changing your life situations and circumstances by the power of His mighty hand in your life. With His own hand He will begin to close doors, halt certain levels of opportunities, end unfruitful and unproductive relationships, dry up territory around you, and block off previous pathways. Then with his favor He will begin to give you new experiences, open new and exciting doors with new levels of opportunities, and introduce you to new people in new places, and then you will know that it is time to pivot in a new direction.

Be Led by the Spirit of God

The Holy Spirit will guide you into truth and the direction you should go. If it is your flesh telling you to turn, it will be for selfish reasons, material gain, perhaps to please others, personal fame, etc. The Holy Spirit is the complete opposite. He will always guide and lead you in a direction that will magnify God, benefit others, enhance your life and serve the surrounding communities. Jesus guaranteed the Holy Spirit would be within us to teach, guide, warn, instruct, strengthen, etc. For it is He, the Holy Spirit, that helps to communicate the sentiments of God and the thoughts of God for the purpose of guiding believers. The Holy Spirit will never steer you opposite of God's will nor will He steer you in conflict to God's will. If the Spirit is urging you to turn, turn around, or turn back, trust Him! He knows what He is talking about. The Holy Spirit is your Greatest Helper on earth.

Your encounter with crossroads, intersections, and junctions can mean that is it time to turn. Are you ready? Are you excited? Well, I am excited for you because I know that God has something marvelous and wonderful ahead should you take that next turn.

Chapter 4

Saul (Paul)

It is Time to Stop

We have discovered that God brings us to crossroads of all sorts; intersections that transition us as well as junctions that connect us to what God has planned and purposed. Looking at both Abram in chapter two and Moses in chapter three of this book, we see how important it is to respond appropriately at each point in the road. Abram discovered at Haran (a crossroad) that when God says move, then move. That was the most befitting response for where God was trying to take him next. Then Moses found out at Pi Hahiroth, between Migdol and the Red Sea, that they would have to make one of the most important turns in their lives according to God's instructions. Abram nor Moses could not argue or fuss about it. It was a well-timed decision that would place them closer to the center of God's will. Also, there are times when God will bring you to other obligatory points on the road to destiny wherein He will most assuredly stop you before opening doors. In some instances, God will stop you to point or set you in the right direction as it pertains to His will. God will take time out in particular seasons to deactivate everything you were doing before and to get your attention to what is next. I have experienced and discovered that our God will stop us in our tracks for many reasons essential for where He is taking you and I. Here are several reasons:

To shape and conform us to the image Jesus Christ.

Sometimes it is to discipline or correct us in an area of our lives.

It could be for the purpose of drawing us closer unto Himself.

To fine tune our ears to hear His voice better.

To improve our eyesight to recognize His hand in our lives.

There may be a need for an attitude adjustment before pressing onward.

Many times it is to give us greater revelation, wisdom, and insight.

To get us in alignment or realignment with what He has in mind for us.

Maybe you are too busy for God, and He wants your undivided attention.

Whatever the reason or reasons, trust me, God will make it clear why He stopped you! Whenever God brings you to a crossroad, intersection, or junction in life, if God intervenes to stop you suddenly, think it not strange! So, let me remind you again, even when God directs you to stop or He puts a halt to your life's current schedule, it is for your good and greater is ahead. It is always for a substantial and more sizeable blessing. Crossroads compel you stop abruptly and perhaps that is what God desires you to do at certain segments in your life. Take heed, obey and stop!

Has God ever just stopped you where you stood? Well, He stopped me in my tracks several times. Yes, He did! It was time. Time for what you might ask? Time for a change, time for redirection, time for renewal, and a reset in my life. I was minding my own business, doing my own thing, thinking all was well and good to go, then suddenly God shut it all down. Whatever I was doing at the time, the Lord brought it to a conclusion. I had never experienced such stoppage before in my life and little did I know at the time that God had brought me to another crossroad. In my earlier days in Christ, spiritually, I had veered off the road having lost my way and I began to drift further and further away from the Lord without realizing it in that instant.

The Lord allowed me to go so far before bringing me to a standstill to deal with me in a more personal and intimate way. He was about to redirect my path. God was about to shorten the season. He was in the process of recalibrating my blessings, opportunities, and activities. God brought me to a complete stop in the road to get my attention and to redirect my path. Whenever you drift away from God, He will bring you to certain markers on the highway of life that will coerce you to stop. I am a witness and not one time during the process did God hurt me, it was all done in love. I think of Saul (Hebrew name) better known as Paul (Roman name) in the New Testament at this juncture.

Saul, whom we know as Paul in the New Testament, had a related situation whereby God stopped him on the road called Damascus. Paul was at a crossroad and God was about to shake things up for him and change his life forever. Let's take a closer look at what happened that fateful day:

But Saul, still breathing threats and murder against the disciples of the Lord, went to the high priest and asked him for letters to the synagogues at Damascus, so that if he found any belonging to the Way, men, or women, he might bring them bound to Jerusalem. Now as he went on his way, he approached Damascus, and suddenly a light from heaven shone around him. And falling to the ground, he heard a voice saying to him, "Saul, Saul, why are you persecuting me?" And Saul said, "Who are you, Lord?" And he said, "I am Jesus, whom you are persecuting. But rise and enter the city, and you will be told what you are to do." (Acts 9:1-6)

Saul was going about his personal agenda: arresting, threatening, harassing, and hounding the Lord's followers. He loathed those of "The Way" movement (early believers), and set out every day to persecute them. He wanted to topple every one of them and sought to bring them in chains to Jerusalem. In Acts 8, Saul was in complete agreement with the killing of Stephen. The story goes that a great wave of persecution of believers in Jesus Christ began that day, sweeping over the church in Jerusalem. Acts 8:3 (paraphrasing) says Saul was like a wild man, made havoc on the church, entering private homes, and dragging out men and women alike and putting them in prison.

As Saul was getting close to the city of Damascus on his mission to knock down, pull down, and tear down the church that started to emerge there, a brilliant light from heaven shone down upon him. It was the Jesus Christ who stopped Saul in the middle of his route and routine. The Bible says Saul fell to the ground and he heard a voice saying to him, "Saul, Saul, why are your persecuting me?" Saul said, "Who are you Lord?" The voice answered very bold and clear, "I am Jesus, the one you are persecuting!" The Lord then instructs Saul to get up from the ground and go into the city and wait for further instructions. Just like that! The Lord in essence told Saul, "STOP!"

The men traveling with Saul that day stood there in utter shock and were speechless. They heard the sound of someone's voice but did not know what the voice was saying, nor did they see anyone. Thus, Saul gets up from the ground but when he opens his eyes, he cannot see anything. He was blinded from the light. Saul had to be led by hand into the city (Damascus) and for three days he was visually impaired and did not eat or drink anything (ref. Acts 9:7-9).

As we have already discussed, God uses crossroads, intersections, and junctions for many reasons.

Sometimes He uses them to simply stop you and I for His intended purpose. As a born-again believer you must get to a place where you can appreciate and embrace certain junctions in the road and stop looking for detours and exit signs each time it does not go your way directionally. God literally brought Saul to a road to stop him. Life as he knew it before inflicting pain and suffering on the church ended that day. Saul's plans suddenly concluded. Without a heads-up, Jesus Christ terminated the former season of Saul. The Damascus Road experience is our experience as well. When God brings us to a stop sign, He really means business with you and me.

Crossroads, intersections, and junctions are no joke in God's economy, especially when He is trying to direct you to stop.

I have learned over the years in my walk with God to take heed to His signals and to obey in the following ways:

Seriously

That is to consider it important enough to drop your agenda for His plans. God knows exactly what lies ahead and around the corner. His wisdom is infinite, so take His gestures seriously (ref. Psalm 147:5).

Soberly

Think, 'I am going to end strong to begin even stronger'. You will need a clear mind, free from the enemy's accusations and lies about your future to stay focused in the present (ref. I Peter 5:8).

Meditatively

Set your affection on things above, and not on things on the earth (Colossians 3:2).

Remember, God has substantially more for you than where you are! Ponder His word, reflect on His promises, remember His commands, and consider His ways over and against your own.

Earnestly

The road that leads to Damascus (the highway that finally brings you to a stop) means God is all business and no play. You will need to be committed to the process and fully in support of the hand of God at work in, around, through, and for you. Be dedicated to the change that is about to come. It is a good thing that is about to happen (ref. Philippians 1:6).

Prayerfully

Remain prayerful. God stopping you at this point does not mean the end of the world. I know that you have heard me say this several times already and I'm going to say it again, God is redirecting you to a new and different place and purpose and there lies the motivation to continue to pray without worrying about things (ref. Philippians 4:6).

Without Hesitation

As you recall, Jesus used a light from heaven to signal Saul to stop! Saul, without hesitation stopped and fell to the ground. God got his attention in a radical and extreme way. He knew exactly what it would take to prompt Saul to his knees before Him. Listen! The moment God gives you the cue, the alert, an indicator, or a wave to stand still, do it without hesitation. The quicker your response, the quicker you will be able to get up from His discipline and move on to what is next as it pertains to His purpose (ref. Hebrews 12:5-11).

Back to Saul. He had to be led by hand into the city of Damascus and for three days he was blinded from the light that flashed around him from heaven, and he did not eat or drink anything (ref. Acts 9:7-9). God got his attention! Now Saul is exactly where God needs him to be: serious, sober, meditative, earnest, prayerful, and without hesitation, waiting with great expectation to hear God's next move.

From Damascus Road to Victory Road:

"Now there was a disciple at Damascus named Ananias. The Lord said to him in a vision, "Ananias." And he said, "Here I am, Lord." And the

Lord said to him, "Rise and go to the street called Straight, and at the house of Judas look for a man of Tarsus named Saul, for behold, he is praying, and he has seen in a vision a man named Ananias come in and lay his hands on him so that he might regain his sight." But Ananias answered, "Lord, I have heard from many about this man, how much evil he has done to your saints at Jerusalem. And here he has authority from the chief priests to bind all who call on your name." But the Lord said to him, "Go, for he is a chosen instrument of mine to carry my name before the Gentiles and kings and the children of Israel. For I will show him how much he must suffer for the sake of my name." So, Ananias departed and entered the house. And laying his hands on him he said, "Brother Saul, the Lord Jesus who appeared to you on the road by which you came has sent me so that you may regain your sight and be filled with the Holy Spirit." And immediately something like scales fell from his eyes, and he regained his sight. Then he rose and was baptized; and taking food, he was strengthened." (Acts 9:10-19)

God will never take you from one road without having another road ready for you. Look at what God had set in place while He was preparing Saul for greater things ahead, and He does the same for you:

1. God prepares *people* - Ananias sent to fellowship and assist Saul.

2. God prepares *places* - Saul resided in the house of Judas.

3. God prepares *platforms* - Saul's new ministry to the Gentiles.

4. God gives *potential* to perform - Saul filled with the Holy Spirit.

5. God gives *power of sight* - Saul regained his sight.

6. God gives *perspective* afresh - Saul was baptized.

7. God gives *provision* - Saul eats and regains strength.

8. God gives *proof* - Saul shares the testimony of his conversion.

What if Saul did not stop on the road leading to Damascus as the Lord had constrained him?

- He would have missed the Lord.

- He would have not been filled with the Holy Spirit.

- He would have never gained necessary revelation.

- He would have forfeited his calling.

- He would have missed out on one of the most exciting journeys of his life.

- He would have continued on a path to destruction.

- He would not have had such a testimony at the end of his days.

Paul, formerly known as Saul, went from the chief of sinners to the Lord's Apostle. Paul saw the world. He met people from everywhere, preached to crowds he never imagined, mentored, and discipled sons and daughters in the Lord. He built churches, traveled extensively, healed and helped thousands with what little he had. He wrote over one third of the New Testament, became known for being a praying man and stood before kings. He became a high-profile leader in the House of the Lord and played an integral part of laying the foundation of the teachings of the church then and for centuries to come. All I can say is, "Thank you, Paul, for heeding to the Lord that fateful day on the road to Damascus." He could have kept going but he stopped, and/or the Lord stopped him. God uses crossroads, intersections, and junctions to bring you and I to a stop in our lives for a very specific purpose in mind. When you discern or perceive the stop sign, the appropriate response is to pause or come to a halt before you decide to proceed.

From one road to the next road:

Well, my friend, God has it all set up and ready for you. He is putting the right people in position just for you. God is setting up special places made just for you. He is constructing platforms for greater opportunities just for you. He has already given you His Holy Spirit and the spiritual gifts to perform what is next in your life. God is healing you spiritually, physically, emotionally, mentally, and financially. Yes! He is bringing the healing you will need to function more effectively and efficiently. When you are stopped it is not in vain. God is giving you a fresh perspective and supplying you with all the provisions necessary to accomplish His purpose. When it has been fully demonstrated in your life, God will give you the opportunity, a personal testimony, and a story to tell that will encourage and strengthen others.

I am excited for you and waiting with great anticipation for your WOW experience! Remember, God will never transition you from one road (Damascus Road) without having another road ready for you. He has a perfect track record of taking people from where they are to victory road.

Chapter 5

The Holy Spirit

Crossroad Signs and Signals

Now we have come to a place where it is paramount to acknowledge the Holy Spirit's presence, ministry, and work in our life experiences when we come across various crossroads, intersections, and junctions in life. We don't hear much about the Holy Spirit's role in the 21st Century, perhaps due to our usage and reliance on technology and gadgetry in our every day lives. Technology is a valuable source used to monitor the quality of air, water, food, education, businesses, military, transportation, etc. Technology is also being used to help the Body of Jesus Christ (the Church) to lift up the name of Jesus. Technology has changed our lives mostly in a positive way but also in a negative way. It is unfavorable when we rely on its mechanisms and engineering more than the Holy Spirit. I thank God for what technology brings to our every day living; however, technology falls short when it comes to the role of the Holy Spirit in the believer's life. The Holy Spirit is our Greatest Helper on earth. He is not at the crossroads in our lives to censure, condemn, or find fault. Rather, He is there willing and able to help us. I learned this at a particular crossroad in my life a few decades ago after several spiritual collisions. Looking back, I sure have had my share of spiritual bumps and accidents on the way to my place of purpose. But God! I recall onlookers and eyewitnesses at the crash site ridiculing and mocking me. They didn't even so much attempt to patch up the wounds I sustained. It goes to say those closest to you can be your greatest detractors and belittlers at various designed intersections. Keep your expectations of others in its proper place so that it does not throw you off your divine trajectory.

Many kicked me while I was down, punished me for failing, sentenced me to mediocrity, and pronounced doom for the poor choices I made.

They did not view me as a young servant preacher trying his best to please his Savior. No mercy or grace was ministered, just judgment. They sat me down on the 'mourner's bench' (which isn't biblical), for all to see me in my shame. But listen ladies and gentlemen, we thank God the Father, the Son, and the Holy Spirit for being nothing like our critics who vilify us at certain points in the road to our destiny. It was during that time that I discovered how different the Holy Spirit was from church folks. The Holy Spirit didn't condemn, ridicule, and never once disgraced me regarding my past downfalls. Instead, He helped me. The Holy Spirit came to my aid to bestow a helping hand and gave me all the assistance I needed to get to where I should be as it pertained to the will of God for my life. He is neither a condemner of men nor a prosecutor of the believers, but He is our Greatest Helper and supporter on earth. The Holy Spirit wants us to succeed in the place where God is taking us. All I could do is be glad and rejoice when the Holy Spirit took me and propped me up.

"For a righteous man falleth seven times, and rises up again: but the wicked fall into mischief." (Proverbs 24:16)

When you come to a crossroad, intersection, or junction on the highway of life, the Holy Spirit is always there to hold up a sign or give you the proper signal you will need to make the next move. The Holy Spirit acts like a policeman or signalman at each turning point you come to in order to help you maneuver. His role is important especially at such a critical spot where tough decisions must be made. How exciting is that? You are at a crossroad, which means you know God is about to take you somewhere greater and you have the Holy Spirit there willing and ready to tell you exactly what to do. However, just as you would obey the signalman or the policeman's command at the intersection on the roadway in the natural, it is as equally important to obey the Holy Spirit's cues and nods He gives you in the spiritual realm. You can depend and rely on Him to do what He was sent to do by the Father and that is to help. He helps us in several ways to get from point A to point B.

He Guides

The Holy Spirit will lead the way if you allow Him. He will never leave you alone to figure out how to navigate your way and to keep you from getting lost on your way to destiny (ref. John 16:13).

He Abides

The Holy Spirit will always continue with you no matter how rough things get at every intersection. Whether you feel His presence or not, He is always there to help you get to the place where God ordained for you to be. You will arrive safely (ref. John 14:16).

He Assures

The Holy Spirit will affirm and validate you when there is doubt in your heart about things He has spoken to you. Days when you are running on empty and you need encouragement, the Holy Spirit will always be present at each juncture to cheer you on through the good times and the bad times. He will remind you of every promise God made to you regarding His plans (ref. 1 Corinthians 2:9-10).

He Teaches

The Holy Spirit will prepare you as you proceed toward your divine destiny. At every crossroad there are lessons and things that you will need to learn before you arrive to your place of purpose. His ministry is to equip you for what the Father has prepared. Who does that? The Holy Spirit. Relish Him, embrace Him, and go with Him because He is getting you primed for a divine purpose (ref. John 14:26).

He Strengthens

The Holy Spirit is strengthening you at each turning point in the road. He does not wait until you get to your place of promise before He bolsters you with His power. He does it at the various crossroads you encounter. He will give you increased strength and more for where He is taking you next. You will need more power and energy than your last assignment and the Holy Spirit is there to ensure that (ref. Ephesians 3:16, 20).

He Empowers

The Holy Spirit gives you the authority to operate on the Father's behalf where He is calling you. He is the one that gives you the official notice to flow in the next undertaking of your life. The Holy Spirit must put that commission in your spirit. He teaches you how to walk with such a God-given authority. You will not need permission to work or function at the next level (ref. Acts 1:8).

He Warns

The Holy Spirit will give you a notification or an alert when there is danger ahead or when conditions have changed as you make your way closer to the center of God's will. You will encounter emergency situations, accidents, and changes in the road. The Holy Spirit is there to forewarn and assist you in getting around detours. There may even be times on the journey when you feel a need to put in a 911 call to God. There will be times when you feel something isn't right or sense there is danger ahead. In a very real sense that is God talking to you through the promptings of the Holy Spirit (ref. Matthew 6:13).

He Gives Joy

The Holy Spirit will give you joy and jubilation on the way. He gives you peace at the crossroad. God desires that you be filled with joy, peace, and happiness on the journey to the Promised Land. May the Holy Spirit fill you with an expectation and exhilaration at every crossroad, intersection, and junction. You do not have to go into the next season depleted of joy. He gives you joy for the journey no matter how long it takes you to get to your God-given destination. Don't wait to be happy; embrace where you are (at the crossroad) and be even happier when you arrive (ref. John 14:27; 16:33).

That is the role of the Holy Spirit in our lives. Acknowledge, embrace, rely, and trust Him to get you from where you are to where you need to be on time. He is your Greatest Helper.

How to recognize when the Holy Spirit is giving you certain signals and cues. PAY ATTENTION! There will be a:

Confirmation

The Holy Spirit will speak clearly to you and specifically through the Word of God, in your daily circumstances, your conscious, or other people. He will communicate by corroborating His Word in your day-to-day activities. Confirmation also comes in various ways including people, convictions, sermons, just to name a few.

If you are concentrating and trusting the Holy Spirit's guidance, He will confirm the truth of His Word. Notice in the text how the Holy Spirit spoke more than once to give Paul confirmation on what direction he needed to go to spread the gospel of Jesus Christ:

"And they went through the region of Phrygia and Galatia, having been forbidden by the Holy Spirit to speak the word in Asia. And when they had come up to Mysia, they attempted to go into Bithynia, but the Spirit of Jesus did not allow them. So, passing by Mysia, they went down to Troas. And a vision appeared to Paul in the night: a man of Macedonia was standing there, urging him, and saying, "Come over to Macedonia and help us." And when Paul had seen the vision, immediately we sought to go on into Macedonia, concluding that God had called us to preach the gospel to them." (Acts 16:6-10)

The Holy Spirit will confirm directions and directives at each junction and intersection in the road that will lead you closer to the center of God's will.

Affirmation

The Holy Spirit will communicate to foster an assurance and a greater sense of certainty that you would know beyond a shadow of doubt that He is ordering your steps in His Word.

Affirmation is when the Holy Spirit keeps repeating Himself to you so it is engrained in your heart until there is little to no fear in the way He is telling you to go. The Holy Spirit will bring to our remembrance His directives over and over again. It will require that you pay attention and do not let it go in one ear and out the other just because it is a reminder of the same instructions.

David told us by way of his personal experience of the affirmation of God:

"Order my steps in thy word: and let not any iniquity have dominion over me." (Psalm 119:133)

You get to where you need to be as the Holy Spirit begins to affirm and guide you by the Word of God.

Inspiration

Once you are assured and confirmed by the Holy Spirit's directions, He will begin to inspire you with the promises of God. The Holy Spirit will begin to give you new things to look forward to on the way to your destination. He will begin to bless you with an expectation and excitement about things to come. The Holy Spirit will build you up and set your soul on fire (passion) with things that God is about to do. My friend, this is what you call 'enjoying the journey'. God wants you and I to experience the joy of the Lord to our destiny. The Holy Spirit gives us the inspiration (fuel) to make it. Notice how God inspired the prophet Isaiah with one promise after another:

"Remember the former things of old: for I am God, and there is none else; I am God, and there is none like me, Declaring the end from the beginning, and from ancient times the things that are not yet done, saying, My counsel shall stand, and I will do all my pleasure: Calling a ravenous bird from the east, the man that executes my counsel from a far country: yea, I have spoken it, I will also bring it to pass; I have purposed it, I will also do it." (Isaiah 46:9-11)

God cannot lie. His promises will energize you from one turning point to the next until you reach and complete your new venture.

Revelation

The unveiling of God's revelation is not so much a prediction of things to come, but it is divine far-sightedness or foresight into what lies ahead as it pertains to God's will for your life. Do not despise what the Holy Spirit imparts to you by way of His revelations.

The Holy Spirit will start divulging specific details about people, places, times, plans, plots, projects, seasons, locations, and so much more. The revelations are for you to think and contemplate how to move forward.

As you continue to grow in the Lord, the closer you get to God, the more He will reveal things to you.

Look what Jesus said to His disciples:

"Henceforth I call you not servants; for the servant knows not what his lord doeth: but I have called you friends; for all things that I have heard of my Father I have made known unto you. (John 15:15)

The Lord reveals more about Himself, His plans, and purposes as you draw nigh to Him. Your proximity to God will always determine what you hear and see. From servant to friend means an intimacy has developed between you and the Lord. He will then begin to share greater insight and revelation into things according to His will. Pat yourself on the back at this juncture! You're making great progress.

Demonstration

How do you recognize the Holy Spirit is giving you certain signals and cues? Once again, He will give you confirmation, affirmation, inspiration, revelation, and then there will be a demonstration of everything that was spoken and revealed to you. You will know that He is leading and guiding you at each crossroad, intersection, and junction in your life. When He brings things to pass and it is manifested before your very eyes, you will see the Lord's mighty power working things out according to what He purposed. It is the Holy Spirit that helps you to this point and He will also lead you into even greater things. Moses declared the demonstration of the hand of God in his life:

"O Lord GOD, thou hast begun to shew thy servant thy greatness, and thy mighty hand: for what God is there in heaven or in earth, that can do according to thy works, and according to thy might?" (Deuteronomy 3:24)

God always illustrate, substantiate, or fulfill every promise and word spoken to you in His own time. You are blessed when you see the hand of God at work in your life because many people miss or disregard Him at work. PAY ATTENTION to the Holy Spirit's communications, confirmations, affirmations, inspirations, and revelations at each crossroad you come to. There will always be a demonstration of His presence and power in your daily life experiences. WATCH AND SEE! I am excited for you. You are not going to crash in this season. You are going to hold the line at the present crossroad you find yourself. I trust that you are going to journey well.

Now let's observe additional signs and signals of the Holy Spirit when encountering crossroads, intersections, and junctions from a spiritual perspective.

Chapter 1 -   God told the Israelites going back to Egypt was not an option.

Chapter 2 -   God told Abraham to move.

Chapter 3 -   God told Moses to turn.

Chapter 4 -   God told Saul (Paul) it is time to stop.

These were cues, gestures, alerts, warnings, and indicators given to God's leaders and his children when they finally came to that place in the road. The Holy Spirit had different instructions for each of them based upon what He had prepared for their lives. The same goes for us. We must pay attention to how the Holy Spirit is prompting us to move at each crossroad.

There are signs and signals by the Holy Spirit that you might encounter at a particular crossroad, intersection, or junction in life:

Yield

At various crossroads in our lives the Holy Spirit may signal you to yield. To yield means to slow down and surrender the right-of-way to God's plan. Oftentimes we want to press the accelerator on God without observing, discerning, or praying about it before we proceed. You must yield the right-of-way to the things that God is speaking and revealing to you before you cross the yield line. So, if you sense the

Holy Spirit indicating you to yield, do not get discouraged and quit. It simply means God has more to reveal or grant before you advance further. With caution proceed and yield only when it is prudent to do so.

Stay the course. Be encouraged. Nothing bad is going to happen to you. Yield signs at spiritual crossroads are standard.

Do Not Enter

You may encounter a do not enter sign in a particular season of your life. Remember the Holy Spirit is there to lead, guide, and signal you as you make your way to the center of God's will. A do not enter road sign from the Holy Spirit means you must not proceed. Obedience is better than sacrifice. Why? At this point in the road the Holy Spirit is circumventing a head-on collision with things and people that may be coming towards you. You and I will save ourselves much heartache and pain if we would heed this sign in the road the first time around. It is the enemy that wants to cause a great collision by sending people and situations to crash into you and hinder the progress you have made. Do not be surprised if you begin to encounter people and circumstances coming at you instead of going with you. They are the opposing traffic sent to deliberately crash into God plans. In addition, follow the instructions and do not enter the posted area. The Holy Spirit will make another way for you to continue your journey safely.

Don't you dare think about uprooting at this point. You must hold your ground until further notice. Expect do not enter signs as the Holy Spirit sojourns with you.

Wrong Way

Here is the truth of the matter: we all get off track. No one is exempt from getting lost on the way to their destination. It happens to the best of us. As a human being we lose sense of navigation for ascertaining our position and following the Holy Spirit's route for our lives. It does not mean you are any less spirit-filled or lacking in some area. It is simply normal, and you should not beat yourself up if you happen to end up on the wrong road. The Holy Spirit will give you a road sign that reads wrong way. It means you are headed in the wrong direction and the Holy Spirit is trying to forewarn you before you get too far out of the way. How can you tell if you are heading in the wrong direction?

1. You will sense in your spirit a wrong way alert indicating an error regarding your directions.

2. By a simple error of accidently turning in the wrong direction, remember as human beings we are prone to make mistakes.

3. God will send people. They may be a parent, a friend, your pastor, your spouse, etc., with good intentions to let you know that you are going the wrong way.

4. Lack of inward peace. Whenever you and I veer off, the Holy Spirit is there to whisper in our ear this is the way. We can be assured He will put us back on track. The Holy Spirit is there to re-direct you without finding fault.

Wrong way signals are customary and you should take them seriously.

U-Turn

Crossroads, intersections, and junctions from a spiritual perspective means that God is about to do something great again in your life. He is going to change your course of direction for a particular season. The Holy Spirit acts more so as a signalman or policeman to let you know the type of turns or maneuvers you are going to be required to make. Easier said than done, right? At each crossroad you should be gaining more experience in time. You should be procuring a familiarity when coming to a crossroad in life. Simultaneously, there should be less panic, stress, worry, and more trusting God at the crossroads of life. You must trust the Holy Spirit's signs, signals, gestures, motions, and indicators no matter what He might help you to do. Sometimes the Holy Spirit will prompt you to make a U-turn as well. U-turns refer to performing a 180-degree rotation to reverse your direction of travel. A U-turn means facing or moving in the opposite direction. One understands this as a driver on the road, but many in the Body of Christ will avoid a U-turn sign in the spiritual realm due to lack of experience, understanding or unwillingness. However, when you see, hear or sense the Holy Spirit directing you to make a U-turn, it may mean there is something that needs revisiting before going any further. It is common for the Holy Spirit to take one in the opposite way or to reverse your direction for several reasons:

- A lesson to learn.

- A mess that needs to be cleaned up.

- A spiritual lesson that needs to be revisited.

- Mend a relationship.

- Go back to school.

- Get out of debt.

- Work on your credit.

- Work on your resume.

- Get closer to God.

- Get your priorities straight.

- Improve your health.

- Improve your prayer life.

- Spend more time with family.

- Re-evaluate your friendships.

As you can see these are very practical reasons why the Holy Spirit will prompt us to make a U-turn in our lives. That is not a bad thing at all. God is up to something amazing in your life. There are legal U-turns permitted by the Holy Spirit, and there are illegal U-turns when a believer does it on their own validity. A U-turn is only permitted at certain times in the natural as well as the spiritual realm.

Praise God for the U-turns in our lives. God wants to reinforce in you His will and His ways so that you won't forget U-turns, signs or signals are normal.

Slow Down

Here is another road sign you must understand as you press forward: slow down. Crossroads in life tells us that there are intersections ahead on your spiritual journey. Be vigilant and slow down because you never know what lies ahead. It is the role of the Holy Spirit to motion us to slow down when necessary.

Sometimes we can be on the fast track and end up ahead of God. Getting ahead of God leads to anticipating God's next move. It is one thing to expect a move from God and it is a whole different ballgame to anticipate God's next move. With great expectations I know that God is going to do something. As Christians we are admonished never to predict what He is going to do next. Instead, we are exhorted to wait on His next move in our lives. While we may be fast on our feet, we will need to slow down in our spirit to understand the vision God is preparing for the season to come.

Do not grow impatient, but let God develop greater patience when you see the slow down sign. God will get you where you need to be next and on time. There is no need to worry at this stage.

Finally, you will see or discern the sign posting that reads bump in the road as you press towards your destiny. It is a common indicator that you should be aware of. The Holy Spirit will forewarn you of life's many bumps as you travel to your destiny.

The sign lets you know there are problems that will arise and will interfere with forward progress. Also, the sign serves as a reminder that no intersection or roadway is without something trying to impede, delay, hamper, or even hinder the progress.

Here is the good news, you will be fine. You will get past every jolt and thump. Bumps in the road are usually not that serious from a spiritual standpoint unless you allow them to hamper your progression. Take it as it comes, bumps are normal. Keep it moving and watch God give you a clear and unobstructed passage into the next season.

Remember, when you come to a crossroad, intersection, or junction on the highway of life, the Holy Spirit is always there to hold up a sign or give you the signal you will need to make the next move. The Holy

Spirit acts like a policeman or signalman at each turning point you come to. His role is important especially when critical decisions must be made. How exciting is that?

Thank you, Holy Spirit, for all that you do to get me where I need to be in the will of God for my life!

I can confidently say that the Holy Spirit has assisted me at many crossroads in my life. I did not always understand His promptings, and I didn't always heed His cautions. In those times the journey towards destiny became more challenging than what God had intended for me. Overtime, I had to grow up in faith, mature in character, and trust God all the more. I learned with the help of the Holy Spirit to depend on His cues because He really does know what He is doing. The Holy Spirit always got me where I needed to be as it pertained to the will of God. Today, I am enjoying the journey, taking the bumps as they come. Turning, stopping, moving, etc., to the Holy Spirit's guidance.

Crossroads, intersections, and junctions have become a place of great inspiration without fear because it is the place where I know that God is up to something great and spectacular. I'm praying that you are enjoying the journey no matter where you are in the process. In Jesus' name. Amen.

Chapter 6

Joshua

It is Time to Cross over

Well, you made it this far. The time has come for you to cross over to the other side. You have endured and been through a lot, but look at you now. No one ever promised that the road leading to your purpose and the promises of God would be easy, but you made it intact. You are complete and you are whole. You are unharmed and unbroken. Perhaps you are marked with some bumps and bruises, but you are not damaged. Despite traffic conditions, bends in the road, various road junctions, oncoming traffic, maybe even a couple of crashes on the way to the Promised Land, yet you survived it. You pulled through by the grace of God with the help and power of the Holy Spirit. Now you are at the place of crossing from one side to the other. You obeyed all the signs and signals the Holy Spirit gave you and with that comes great rewards and blessings from God the Father, through the Jesus Christ. Through it all, I've made it. With the Coronavirus still on the rise and Omicron variant having emerged last fall taking over the Delta virus, it inundated the United States as of 2020. The tragic death of George Floyd and so many others in our Black and Brown communities sparked protests all over the world. Not to mention under the current Biden administration police brutality and reform remains elusive. In addition, the recent mass shooting at a supermarket in Buffalo, New York was a tragic racist attack that took the lives of ten people. On

May 24, 2022, a gunman targeted a 4th grade class at an elementary school in Uvalde, Texas killing nineteen students and two teachers, and wounding seventeen others. It was the deadliest school shooting in America since Sandy Hook in 2012. Gas prices are at an all-time high. According to the news, Russia officially declared to be at war with Ukraine as of May 9, 2022. Simultaneously, China threatened a full-scale war and a nuclear response to the United States and Japan if they interfered in China's handling of Taiwan. The increase in oil prices, groceries, clothes, mortgages, rent, and healthcare, just to name a few, is proving to be a formidable challenge to millions of Americans who are still recovering from the pandemic. Food banks and other assistance programs are experiencing low supplies. The devil is busy, but God is still in control.

While you cannot ignore the distresses and disasters going on in the World, you cannot afford to miss the next move of God in your life. Crisis, calamities, and catastrophes, etc., are happening in the land. A divine season is upon us and change is inevitable. As we cross over from one side to the other, shifting is taking place on all levels:

- Globally

- Nationally

- Locally

- Politically

- Corporately

- Financially

- Ministerially

- Individually

- Personally

- Spiritually

Here is the good news of the gospel! What is coming is far more extraordinary than the former things. Are you excited about this season of your life? After years of preparation, dedication, and commitment to discipleship and personal growth under the influence of the Holy Spirit, God's purpose and plan is being fulfilled. With each interchange you will experience a variety of emotions, but with the assistance of the Holy Spirit you will persevere.

Nostalgia

Is defined as a sentimental longing or wishful affection for the past, typically for a period or place with happy personal associations.

Melancholy

Feelings of sad thoughts, usually related to people, places and locations. Sorrowful, downcast, discouraged about certain disconnections at the point of relocating.

Stress

A physical, chemical or emotional factor that causes bodily or mental tension resulting from factors that tend to alter one's spiritual, mental, physical, and emotional equilibrium.

Anxiety

Anxiety is the mind and body's reaction to stressful, dangerous or unfamiliar situations and places. It is the sense of uneasiness, distress or dread you feel before a significant event.

Doubt

Feelings of uncertainty, hesitancy, suspicion, and insecurity.

Apprehension

Here are the first and second cousins to your feelings of apprehension: tension, nervousness, fidgetiness, misgiving, and panic.

Fear

Fear is an unpleasant emotion caused by the belief that someone or something is likely to cause pain or loss. It is misgiving about situations, people, and places for one reason or another.

With all things considered, allow me to offer some insight at this point. The story is told of old Bishop Warren Chandler, after whom the School of Theology at Emory University was named. As he lay on his deathbed, a friend inquired as to whether he was afraid. "Please tell me frankly," he said, "do you fear crossing over the river of death?" "Why," replied Chandler, "I belong to a Father who owns the land on both sides of the river."

So, I say to you, do not let fear of moving on from one season to the next or one place to the next overwhelm you where you contemplate turning back. Remember chapter one? Going back to Egypt is not an option. You need not to fear crossing over the river of death or any river for that matter. Why? Just like Bishop Chandler you belong to a Father who owns the land on both sides of the river.

Let me also suggest that all these emotional feelings are absolutely and unequivocally normal to the human experience. If you start off scared, it's okay. God will never shun you for experiencing such emotions.

Remember the Promises of God:

"So then faith cometh by hearing, and hearing by the word of God" (Romans 10:17)

"For God hath not given us the spirit of fear; but of power, and of love, and of a sound mind." (2 Timothy 1:7)

"Faithful is he that calleth you, who also will do it." (1 Thessalonians 5:24)

"For it is God which worketh in you both to will and to do of his good pleasure." (Philippians 2:13)

"I can do all things through Christ which strengthens me." (Philippians 4:13)

"Have I not commanded you? Be strong and courageous. Do not be frightened, and do not be dismayed, for the LORD your God is with you wherever you go." (Joshua 1:9)

"Ye are of God, little children, and have overcome them: because greater is he that is in you, than he that is in the world." (1 John 4:4)

No More Practice, it is Performance Time

God told Joshua it is time to cross over to the other side of the Jordan River. The journey begins! I am sure that Joshua, Caleb, Eleazar, and the Children of Israel had mixed emotions about the move as well. In fact, I am sure of it because in almost every chapter in the book of Joshua, God is telling Joshua not to be afraid.

"Have not I commanded thee? Be strong and of a good courage; be not afraid, neither be thou dismayed: for the LORD, thy God is with thee whithersoever you go." (Joshua 1:9)

The time had come for Joshua and the Israelites to cross over from the east side (Wilderness) of the Jordan to the west side (Promised Land) of the Jordan. Practice time was over for them. It was time to perform and act out everything they had been taught by Moses in the wilderness. This included the tribes of Reuben, Gad, and half the tribe of Manasseh who had been promised by Moses the land on the east side of the Jordan. However, they were instructed to help their brothers conquer their territory and to stay with them until they completed the conquest. They were given the green light. School was out, it was time to walk it out:

➤ Go forward

➤ Go further

➤ Face what faces you

➤ Face who is facing you

➤ Without fear

➢ Flourish

➢ Be fruitful

➢ Something good is going to happen

➢ Conquer the land

➢ Occupy the land

There was nothing more to study. No more training in the wilderness nor sitting under Moses' tutelage. God was ready! The question remains, are you ready? This is what it has been all about. This moment right here and now. There comes a time while at the crossroads of life when all that you have learned will be put into action. That time is now! What is about to happen you might ask? GREATER!

"Every place that the sole of your foot will tread upon I have given to you, just as I promised to Moses. From the wilderness and this Lebanon as far as the great river, the river Euphrates, all the land of the Hittites to the Great Sea toward the going down of the sun shall be your territory. No man shall be able to stand before you all the days of your life. Just as I was with Moses, so I will be with you. I will not leave you or forsake you." (Joshua 1:3-5)

Here is what greater looks like:

The gravity of the blessing, "every place."

The vastness of the blessing, "from the wilderness to the Lebanon mountains in the north."

The width of the blessing, "from the Mediterranean Sea in the west to the Euphrates River in the east, including the land of the Hittites."

The duration of the blessing, "all the days of your life."

The intensity of the blessing, "just as I was with Moses, so will I be with you. I will not leave you or forsake you."

Count Down 5, 4, 3, 2, 1

And Joshua commanded the officers of the people, "Pass through the midst of the camp and command the people, 'Prepare your provisions, for within three days you are to pass over this Jordan to go in to take possession of the land that the LORD your God is giving you to possess." And to the Reubenites, the Gadites, and the half-tribe of Manasseh Joshua said, "Remember the word that Moses the servant of the LORD commanded you, saying, 'The LORD your God is providing you a place of rest and will give you this land.' Your wives, your little ones, and your livestock shall remain in the land that Moses gave you beyond the Jordan, but all the men of valor among you shall pass over armed before your brothers and shall help them, until the LORD gives rest to your brothers as he has to you, and they also take possession of the land that the LORD your God is giving them. Then you shall return to the land of your possession and shall possess it, the land that Moses the servant of the LORD gave you beyond the Jordan toward the sunrise." And they answered Joshua, "All that you have commanded us we will do, and wherever you send us we will go. Just as we obeyed Moses in all things, so we will obey you. Only may the LORD your God be with you, as he was with Moses! Whoever rebels against your commandment and disobeys your words, whatever you command him, shall be put to death. Only be strong and courageous." (Joshua 1:10-18)

Remember your Training

Joshua was the new leader, and he begins to prepare the Children of Israel to cross over the great Jordan River to enter the land of Promise. They are right there at the brink of the Jordan, bags packed and set to go, right! In preparation for the "greater things" God had in store for Joshua and the new generation, it was paramount that they remember what they were trained to do back in the wilderness. Moses taught them well, though his instructions did not have much influence on the older generation, the generation after that was ready to run with it. They were pumped up about the next season and they said to Joshua:

"All that you have commanded us we will do, and wherever you send us we will go. Just as we obeyed Moses in all things, so we will obey you. Only may the LORD your God be with you, as he was with Moses! Whoever rebels against your commandment and disobeys your words, whatever you command him, shall be put to death. Only be strong and courageous." (Joshua 1:16-18)

There was no stopping them now! Much of their success would rest in their ability to remember the training they had received while under Moses' tutelage. All their experiences in the wilderness gave them the education they would need in the land of Canaan.

The Children of Israel were trained to occupy, fight and obey the voice of God without hesitancy. Make sure you remember every lesson and the teachings acquired and received by the Holy Spirit. God has given you a sure foundation that is unshakeable and unmovable.

Remember your Trainer

Moses' influence was very evident in their lives. Crossing over to the other side of blessings does not mean forgetting those who helped you along the way. Moses got Joshua and the next generation primed and prepared over a forty-year period. If it were not for Moses' leadership, they would not have made it to the brink of the Jordan, ready to cross to the other side.

Notice the text:

"After the death of Moses, the servant of the LORD, the LORD said to Joshua the son of Nun, Moses' assistant, "Moses my servant is dead. Now therefore arise, go over this Jordan, you and all this people, into the land that I am giving to them, to the people of Israel. Every place that the sole of your foot will tread upon I have given to you, just as I promised to Moses." (Joshua 1:1-3)

Moses is now dead. He has crossed over from death to life eternal. Oh! How easy it is to forget those that deposited within us the wisdom of God's Word. This should not be the case for you and I. Please remember your teachers, mentors, advisers, counselors, and spiritual leaders near and far. Occasionally it helps to recall and reflect upon those who helped you discover God's plan and purpose for your life.

During their days in the wilderness, Joshua and the Children of Israel were admonished not to forget God's word:

"Only be strong and very courageous, being careful to do according to all the law that Moses my servant commanded you. Do not turn from it to the right hand or to the left, that you may have good success wherever you go. This Book of the Law shall not depart from your mouth, but you shall meditate on it day and night, so that you may be careful to do according to all that is written in it. For then you will make your way prosperous, and then you will have good success." (Joshua 1:7-8)

Unlike their forefathers, Joshua and the Children of Israel's prosperity and success depended on them keeping God's word at the forefront of their minds and hearts. As you flourish in the things of God, don't get distracted by the things on the left or right, but allow the Holy Spirit to lead you in this important season of your life. Scripture memorization helps me to remember the truth of God's Word by:

- Writing it down.

- Reciting it often.

- Incorporating it into our prayers.

- Listening to audio Bible messages while driving.

- Immersing myself in the Word of God.

- Trusting the Holy Spirit to bring it back to my remembrance.

- Walking it out by making application of God's principles.

These days, everyone is trying to forget the past, but if you forget the past then you forget your training. You leave behind those that trained you and you omit a plethora of truth that is meant to aid in your current situations and certainly where God is leading you. You will be the greater person, in a greater place, doing greater things!

You are good to go!

When it is time to cross over, the Holy Spirit will give the word. He told Joshua it is time to go:

Then Joshua rose early in the morning, and they set out from Shittim. And they came to the Jordan, he and all the people of Israel, and lodged there before they passed over. At the end of three days the officers went through the camp and commanded the people, "As soon as you see the ark of the covenant of the LORD your God being carried by the Levitical priests, then you shall set out from your place and follow it. Yet there shall be a distance between you and it, about 2,000 cubits in length. Do not come near it, in order that you may know the way you shall go, for you have not passed this way before." Then Joshua said to the people, "Consecrate yourselves, for tomorrow the LORD will do wonders among you." And Joshua said to the priests, "Take up the ark of the covenant and pass on before the people." So, they took up the ark of the covenant and went before the people. (Joshua 3:1-5)

Can you imagine the level of excitement both Joshua and the Children of Israel experienced? Crossroads after crossroads! Intersections after intersections! Junctions after junctions! Now they are at the Jordan

River. God is before them (the Ark of the Covenant) and they were to follow Him through the water. The Lord was about to do wonders among them three days from now according to Joshua 3:2. They received the signal to go!

"Now the priests bearing the ark of the covenant of the LORD stood firmly on dry ground in the midst of the Jordan, and all Israel was passing over on dry ground until all the nation finished passing over the Jordan." (Joshua 3:17)

They are crossing on dry land with the priest and the Ark of the Covenant leading the way. The wilderness is behind them. Egypt is even further behind them. Joshua and the Children of Israel are making application of their training. They are doing it!

"For the priests bearing the ark stood in the midst of the Jordan until everything was finished that the LORD commanded Joshua to tell the people, according to all that Moses had commanded Joshua. The people passed over in haste. And when all the people had finished passing over, the ark of the LORD and the priests passed over before the people." (Joshua 4:10-11)

Now it's your turn, just do it! Several critical decisions must be made:

1. Trust God where you are.

2. Trust God where you are going.

3. Give yourself time to learn your way. You have never been this way before.

4. Be patient with yourself.

5. Reinforce good habits (prayer, worship, and the Word.)

6. Be willing to make adjustments.

7. Stay out of trouble, obey.

8. Give God all the glory and remember this day.

Won't He do it! Watch God do it! Many lessons have been learned. The past is behind you. The future is before you. So it was with Joshua and all his followers, practice time is over. It is performance time in Christ Jesus to the glory of God.

Conclusion

Regroup, Rethink, Repent, and Rejoice

Well! More than this book ever becoming a best seller, it is my prayer that it will be a blessing to all that may read it. It has been my goal from the onset of this project to encourage, enlighten, and equip the Body of Christ and community at large to become better suited when coming to a crossroad, intersection, or junction in life.

I have learned through the years crossroads from a spiritual standpoint is nothing to deplore or to abhor. Instead, crossroads should be viewed as a time to regroup, rethink, and repent from things that have no place where God is taking you next. God forbid, you and I walk into the next season of our lives practicing the same old habits and doing the same old things. Then, we turn around and expect God to do a new thing. You cannot walk through new doors with old ways. Jesus said in the gospels that you cannot put new wine into old wineskins. It does not work that way. So, God brings us to a crossroad to deal with us on a more personal and intimate way. Whenever you encounter a crossroad, it is a time being granted for you to regroup, rethink, and maybe even repent from undertakings that may have hindered you in past times, seasons, and places.

Regroup

It means it is time to mold you into the image of Christ. From time-to-time, we are prone to drift and begin to walk at a distance from God. It happens without even trying and when it does, God brings us to a point in the road where we must face the damage before crossing over into the next season of our lives. God forbid you and I enter the Promised Land with our old, ugly, and unpleasant ways.

Perhaps you've made some mistakes and forfeited many blessings. You realize it now, so regroup. It is time to recalibrate your energy and efforts towards being more fruitful. Crossroads means it is time to regroup.

Rethink

Time to review, revise, and re-examine your heart. You can work on the outside and portray that all is well but really it is not well at all if your heart is in the same place as before. This is an act that is between you and God and it has very little to do with you and others. God deals with the inward (heart and mind) while man looks at the outer (body and material). You can fool man, but you cannot dupe God. The Lord places situations in the road that causes us to have to pull over and take a deep look within our soul. He desires for us to deal with it before going any further. The change that needs to happen lie in your heart and not in your marriage, ministry, or career, etc. It is a time to reconsider those feats of yours to re-evaluate whether they have a place in your future or not. If you do this, you will be in the top percentile of people that allow the Holy Spirit to work within one's own heart and mind; while many will choose to focus on their outer appearance to gain the favor of man rather than God. At each crossroad it is time to rethink whether our deeds and activities are reflective of the heart and do they align with the will of God.

Repent

Crossroads in life give you the time and opportunity to change your course and get back on the right track God has planned for you. Repentance is not a change of behavior as much as it is a change of convictions based upon a change of one's heart and mind. It is at the crossroads of life where God, by the power of the Holy Spirit that works at convincing you (not condemning you) there is a higher and better way motivating you to change direction. Going forward you will discover at this juncture the importance of walking in a manner that is pleasing to God. Thank God that our past, present, and future sins were eradicated at the cross. As forgiven people, it becomes easier to cross over to the other side and be accountable for what God has planned and purposed for our lives.

Rejoice

Rejoice in the Lord: and again, I say, Rejoice. Things are about to change for you. God has new levels and new doors to open for you. He has positioned you so that He may use you in a greater capacity. The journey has been rough, and the going has been tough, but it was all for your preparation. The Lord is about to match you up (perfectly) to your next assignment and blessing. So, wipe your tears, stick out your chest, and hold up your head because you have made it to the place where you need to be for the next major move to take place.

This moment right here and right now is for the best. There is no more room for fear or anxiety at the crossroads of life. Band doubt from your mind, resist turning back to where you came from.

You made it to the brink of the Jordan River so to speak, and now it is time to crossover to the other side.

I know that you may have cried a many of nights, but wipe them tears, and begin to experience the joy that comes at each crossroad, intersections, and junction when you trust God as your Heavenly Father, and Jesus as your personal Lord and Savior.

So, rejoice always and again I say, Rejoice.

Philippians 4:4

This is not the end; you are just getting started afresh.